Digital Legacy
A Guide to Managing Your Social Media Footprint

Table of Contents

We are what we share.

— Charles Leadbeater

Chapter 1. Introduction

In this special report, we explore the fascinating and increasingly crucial realm of 'Digital Legacy,' where we decode the intricacticalities of managing your own social media footprint. This is not about highly technical jargon nor about convoluted concepts. It's about weaving your digital story, leaving a footprint that aligns with your principles and intentions, and efficiently managing your virtual existence. With a delightful blend of expert insights, user-friendly strategies, and practical guidelines, this report is designed to help you be the master of your digital persona. As we dive into this enthralling narrative, you'll discover how to craft, curate, and safeguard your digital legacy effectively. Come, join us on this enlightening journey; get a grasp on your e-footprint and transform your digital interactions. By reading this report, you're taking the first stride towards mastering your virtual life - and who knows, you might just inspire others to do the same!

Chapter 2. Understanding Your Digital Footprint

The digital footprint refers to the trace or record that you involuntarily or voluntarily leave behind in the digital universe through your activities, communications, and transactions carried out on websites, social media, and other web-based platforms. With the advancement of digital technology and its rapid fusion with our daily existence, the digital footprint's magnitude and complexity has grown significantly. However, the understanding of its implications, management, and its associated technical, legal, and ethical issues still remain poorly understood by many.

2.1. The Anatomy of a Digital Footprint

In essence, a digital footprint is a byproduct of digital interactions, transactions, and activities. It's our digital DNA, an indelible imprint left on the digital plane. Your digital footprint can manifest in two ways: passive and active. Passive footprints are generated when data about your activities is collected without your direct intention. This could be your browsing histories, location data, or device information. On the other hand, the active footprint contains information that you choose to share, like your social media posts, comments, shared photos or videos, and other online content.

One fundamental aspect of a digital footprint is that it is practically impossible to erase. Each interaction shapes the digital profile that's visible not only to your selected network but often, to the world at large. This profile is a reflection of your personality, beliefs, preferences, and behaviors.

2.2. The Impact and Influence of Your Digital Footprint

Every data element in your footprint contributes to the digital profile that people, organizations, and algorithms perceive about you. Many people fail to realize that the formation of this profile starts quite innocently – every comment we post, every photo we share, every site we visit, every form we fill out, every app we download, and more.

A digital footprint can be as influential as it is persistent. It forms a significant part of both personal and professional personas. It is used by marketers to target advertisements, by potential employers to make hiring decisions, by educational institutions for admissions and sometimes by law enforcement agencies for investigations. Therefore, being aware of its power is of crucial importance.

2.3. Tracing Your Digital Footprint: A Step Towards Better Management

Understanding and exploring your existing digital footprint is the first step towards better management. Dive deep into your social media profiles, review your posts, comments, photographs, and check-ins. Look for ambiguous posts that can be misinterpreted, randy memes that could be considered offensive, and indications of bias or prejudice that you might have unknowingly exhibited.

Also, search for yourself online. The results can be enlightening, revealing how recruiters, potential partners, or even hackers could see you. Once you've viewed it holistically, you can start formulating your strategies to build a favorable digital footprint that corresponds with your personal or professional goals – a robust descriptor of who you are and who you aspire to be.

2.4. Data Privacy and Your Digital Footprint

With regard to privacy, an indiscriminate approach to digital footprint can pose a risk. Personal information captured within your digital footprint could be misused if it falls into the wrong hands. Data breaches are a serious concern, and your digital footprint can reveal more than you might have intended to.

So, be wary of the information you choose to share. Information like your date of birth, physical address, location checkpoints, and other confidential details should be handled with care. The key is to maintain a balance between exhibiting authenticity and ensuring the necessary precaution against potential data misuse.

As we draw this chapter to a close, it is essential to note that recognizing the potential impact of your digital footprint and taking active steps towards its careful curating and management is today's digital-age need. The choice and control that you exercise over your footprint often mirror the degree of mastery that you hold over your virtual life. A deeper understanding of the content and propagation of your digital footprint forms a pivotal step towards more informed digital conduct, leading to a digitized existence of empowerment, security, and fulfillment.

Chapter 3. Scrutinizing Social Media: Platforms and Their Influence

Social media has blossomed into an integral part of modern life, linking individuals in ways unimaginable just a few decades ago. As we delve into the depths of these dynamic platforms and their compelling influence on our digital footprints, we begin to comprehend their importance and indispensability in shaping our virtual selves and, by extension, our digital legacies.

3.1. Key Social Media Platforms and Their Unique Attributes

There's a diverse range of social media platforms, each with distinctive features and appeal catering to different user preferences and purposes. Three of the most influential platforms include Facebook, Instagram, and Twitter.

Facebook is the juggernaut of social media, with an enormous user base spanning multiple generations. Its core features include posting text statuses, pictures, and videos, alongside integrative functions supporting businesses, groups, and events. Facebook's influence on users' digital footprints is profound, as it provides a vast panorama of one's life, interspersed with personal beliefs, hobbies, professional pursuits, and familial ties.

Instagram, a visually-centric platform, is primarily used for sharing photographs and short videos. Instagram Stories, a feature permitting content visibility for a 24-hour period, allows for ephemeral glimpses into users' lifestyles, frequently showcasing everyday moments. Instagram, therefore, fosters a differently nuanced digital footprint, emphasizing visual aesthetics and serving as a potent tool for personal branding.

Twitter's primary focus rests on text-based 'tweets'. It promotes real-time conversations and community engagement. Twitter's digital footprint embodies more instantaneous and conversational aspects of users' lives, frequently revealing their thoughts and opinions about diverse issues.

3.2. The Influence of Social Media on Your Digital Footprint

Social media's impact on your digital footprint is twofold, affecting both your individual persona and your broader engagement with online communities.

On the personal front, the content you post on social media constructs your digital persona, mirroring your interests, beliefs, and experiences. Whether through a tweet, a Facebook post, or an Instagram Story, every piece of content contributes to an ongoing narrative about who you are, shaping perceptions about your online identity.

On the community level, social media enables engagement and interaction with other users, further influencing your digital footprint. Your comments on others' posts, your shares, your likes, and dislikes, even whom you choose to follow, all inscribe an indelible echo of your virtual self.

3.3. Social Media's Impact on Personal and Professional Lives

With professional platforms like LinkedIn gaining momentum and employers increasingly turning towards social media for hiring, your digital footprint can substantially impact your career. Recruiters often evaluate job applicants' online presence to ascertain their compatibility with company culture, professionalism, and communication skills. Consequently, curating a credible and professional online persona is paramount.

Simultaneously, on the personal front, social media shapes relationships and interactions. Our digital footprints on these platforms provide a sense of social presence, helping us maintain connections, express emotions, or extend support, thus profoundly influencing our social dynamics.

3.4. The Risks and How to Navigate Them

However, social media's influence is not bereft of risks. Oversharing personal information could lead to privacy infringement or identity theft. Additionally, the permanence of online content can pose challenges, where hastily posted content may resurface years later with damaging consequences. It is vital, therefore, to exercise discretion and regularly evaluate your digital footprint on these platforms.

To tackle these challenges, follow a few key strategies:

- Regularly review your privacy settings on each platform to control who has access to your content.

- Take care in the creation and sharing of content - a useful rule of thumb is avoiding posts you would not want a potential employer or a close relative to see.

- Frequently evaluate your list of friends or followers to maintain a quality network that reflects your preferences and standards.

By taking these steps, you can successfully scrutinize and navigate the influence of social media on your digital footprint.

In our digital era, social media representation is inextricably tied to real-world identity. Managing this online presence, therefore, is more than conscientious communication or reputation management. It's the art of weaving your unique digital tapestry, a vivid expression of your individuality that ripples across the virtual world, leaving behind a distinctive digital legacy.

Chapter 4. Creating a Positive Digital Persona

A digital persona is essentially your online self, a cultivated reflection that you project onto the internet. This persona may embody different aspects of your personality, align with your professional ambitions, or even serve as an expression of your various passions. Regardless of the attributes you choose to emphasize, your digital persona plays a pivotal role in the way others perceive you in the virtual world.

4.1. The Importance of a Positive Digital Persona

Before we delve into how to construct a positive digital persona, we must first understand why it plays a crucial role in our digital lives. Your digital persona reflects your personal brand, beliefs, values, or professional expertise. It invigilates how others perceive you through the digital lens. It could be a potential employer doing a quick internet reconnaissance, a distant relative browsing through your social media posts, or a prospective romantic partner trying to glean insight into your character from your online activity. In all these scenarios, a highly regarded digital persona can enhance your credibility, boost your professional prospects, generate trust, and foster meaningful virtual connections.

4.2. Identifying Your Persona

In order to radiate positivity online, you must first identify your digital persona. Start by defining its purpose. Are you striving to enhance your professional image? Perhaps you are an entrepreneur eager to position yourself as an industry expert? Maybe you are an artist keen to showcase your brilliant work to the world? Or, you might even be an activist seeking to propagate a cause dear to your heart. Once you've identified your purpose, tailor your persona to align with your objectives. Remember, granularity lends authenticity: your target audience is likely to connect more meaningfully to a nuanced persona rather than a vague, generic one.

4.3. Curating Your Persona

Once you have identified your persona, the next step is to curate it. Curation here refers to the selective dissemination of content, in addition to its creation. What you choose to share on your digital platforms becomes part of your perceived identity. Strive to maintain a consistent voice and message across your digital footprint. This doesn't mean you have to limit yourself to posting only about one topic, but rather that your posts should reflect your persona's thematic coherence. Use your preferred language tone - be it formal, casual, sardonic, or enthusiastic – across all your digital platforms, further strengthening your digital identity.

4.4. Celebrating Positivity and Kindness

The foundation of a positive digital persona is a genuine commitment to positivity and kindness. In the fast-paced virtual world, it's easy to get embroiled in heated debates or controversial topics. However, maintaining a positive tone, expressing empathy, supporting others, and sharing uplifting content can enhance your esteem in the unforgiving digital landscape. This is not a call for perpetual agreement or universal acceptance, but a nudge towards considerate disagreement and respectful discourse.

4.5. Transparency and Authenticity

These twin towers of digital persona have become increasingly vital in the current digital narrative, with users showing a growing preference for transparent and authentic content. The days of carefully manufacturing every aspect of our digital lives are slowly fading, giving way to an era that celebrates real people and their real lives. Being open about your struggles, successes, and various stages can imbue your digital persona with compelling authenticity, forming deeper connections with your audience.

4.6. Resilience to Digital Negativity

Inevitably, you will encounter digital negativity, in the form of harsh comments, unfavourable reviews, or even online trolls. It's critical to handle these situations with grace and aplomb. Instead of retaliating with hostility, maintain your poise, and take constructive criticism on board. Understand that not everyone will align with your viewpoints, and that is okay. What's more important is how you manage these scenarios.

4.7. The Power of Listening and Engagement

Lastly, a positive digital persona is one that listens and engages. Active interaction with your audience fosters a sense of community, promotes exchange of ideas, and strengthens your online reputation. From timely responses, heartfelt comments, asking for feedback, to initiating relevant discussions, there are numerous ways to engage meaningfully with your digital audience.

In conclusion, building a positive digital persona is an ongoing journey, interleaved with navigation of changing digital dynamics, evolving personal insights, and adaptable social conventions. As the architects of our e-selves, we have the power to shape our virtual presence, communicate our unique stories, and leave enduring digital legacies. By stepping into this role with conscientious intent, you are equipping yourself to transform the digital sphere, one positive interaction at a time.

Chapter 5. Controlling and Curating Your Online Reputation

As digital platforms continue to take over our lives, the need to construct and administer your personal reputation online ever-increasingly becomes apparent. This chapter unfolds, outlining the important steps for controlling and curating your online reputation.

5.1. Understanding Online Reputation

From the moment you first explore the digital world, you begin to establish your online reputation. Every post, every image, every comment, those liked posts, the pages subscribed to, in essence, every digital action contributes to your digital persona. In simple terms, your online reputation is the image, the perception that people form about you when they find you online. This perception is shaped by an immersive collage of your interactions across the array of digital platforms. In contemporary society, where judgments often take shape in split seconds, understanding and managing this reputation becomes a matter of paramount importance.

5.2. The Role of Personal Branding

Personal branding is central to establishing your presence online. Each person, intentionally or unintentionally, curates a brand image that mirrors what they believe in, what they represent. This effectively becomes your fingerprint in the virtual sands of the Internet. You determine the color, theme, language, and flavor of your digital persona. Simply put, personal branding is about using your uniqueness to leave an impression and make a memorable digital trail.

5.3. Tools and Techniques for Controlling Your Online Persona

There exist ample strategies to control one's online persona. To begin with, becoming self-aware of your online actions can significantly improve your digital footprint. Take the time to review your digital actions and their consequences regularly. Subsequently, another effective way would be to undertake an occasional 'digital clean-up'. Scan and analyze your social media accounts and delete posts that do not reflect your current views or brand image. Moreover, consider adjusting privacy settings to act as a buffer for inadvertent digital leakage.

Furthermore, two very crucial components of online reputation management are the design and the consistency of your online persona. Decide the themes, tones, hashtags which define your digital self, and maintain these consistently across platforms. This emphasizes your unique voice in an over-saturated digital space.

5.4. Dealing with Online Negativity

In the digital world, a certain degree of negativity seems virtually inevitable. From harsh comments to misrepresentations, your online reputation might sometimes receive detracting elements. In such circumstances, timely responses are crucial. Act promptly to mitigate negativity, but always maintain your cool and uphold the values you stand for.

Online negativity can present an excellent opportunity for growth and refinement. Always remain open to constructive feedback, allowing your digital persona to evolve dynamically. Use these times as a means to reflect and grow, becoming a better version of your digital self.

5.5. Future-proofing Your Online Reputation

In a fast-paced digital society, it's essential to remain adaptable. Technologies change, social platforms trend and wane, but your overarching responsibility towards your online reputation persists. Continue learning about new platforms, tools, and strategies to keep your digital reputation sparkling. Regular audits, periodic clean-ups, and consistent content curation will ensure that your digital footprint remains evergreen.

Remember, the aim is to weave a digital story that resonates with your real-life persona, embodying your values and aspirations. Control over your digital footprint isn't about hiding your flaws; it's about portraying an honest and enhanced reflection of who you truly are.

To manage your online reputation efficiently, stay patient. The reputation-building process is slow and requires consistent effort. It's your persistent attempts at curating your content, managing your interactions, and controlling your digital persona that will eventually culminate in a wholesome and empowering digital legacy.

In summary, controlling and curating your online reputation entails a nurturing process of careful crafting, deliberate decisions, and conscious digital behaviors. May your digital journey be filled with thoughtful actions that together weave an inspiring digital legacy.

Chapter 6. Secure Your Digital Life: Essential Safety Measures

In the digital age, every bit of personal and professional information that you share online can be remarkably risky if not adequately safeguarded. As technology evolves continually, our exposure to cyber threats significantly increases, highlighting the dire need for adopting a robust digital safety regimen. In this comprehensive chapter, we will navigate the terrain of digital safety, and share the various techniques and tools you can employ to secure your online identity and data.

6.1. Understanding Cyber Threats

Before any discussion of safety measures, it is essential to recognize the potential threats in the online space. Cyber threats can come from a variety of sources and in different forms, such as malware, phishing attacks, data breaches, identity theft, and online scams. They exploit vulnerabilities in your digital affairs, retrieving sensitive information, and can potentially lead to substantial financial loss and reputation damage. Therefore, understanding cyber threats provide the foundation upon which you build your digital security strategy.

6.2. Internet Security Essentials: Antivirus and Firewalls

The first line of defense in securing your digital life is having strong Internet security software. These typically include antivirus and firewall programs intended to prevent, detect, and remove malware.

Antivirus software scans and provides defense against malware, which can infect your devices through harmful links, attachments, or even redistributed software. Up-to-date antivirus software is an absolute non-negotiable aspect of your digital safety measures and should be configured to regularly update for the latest threat definitions.

Firewalls act as a shield between your computer (or network) and the Internet, monitoring all incoming and outgoing traffic. They filter out unrecognized or harmful data and prevent unwanted remote access, thus providing an additional layer of security.

6.3. Secure Password Policies

Next to Internet security software, an efficiently managed password policy is a significant component of safeguarding your digital life. Using strong, unique passwords for each website or online service, bolstered with two-step or multi-factor authentication, can significantly reduce your vulnerability to cyber-attacks.

Creating a unique and complex password can indeed be a daunting task. However, the use of password management tools can aid in generating and storing strong passwords securely. Remember, a robust password policy is not a one-time affair but necessitates an ongoing commitment to security.

6.4. Safe Browsing Habits

Understanding cyber threats and securing your devices and accounts are fundamental steps. However, developing safe online habits is arguably even more crucial. Only visiting trusted websites, refraining from sharing sensitive information online, ever being wary of unexpected emails or messages, and regularly updating your device's operating system and applications can significantly diminish the risk of falling prey to cyber threats.

6.5. Utilizing Private Networks: SSL and VPN

Secure Sockets Layer (SSL) and Virtual Private Network (VPN) provide additional protective measures when you are browsing the internet or communicating online. SSL is a security technology that creates an encrypted link between a web server and a browser, ensuring that all data transferred between remains private. On the other hand, VPNs can hide your IP address and location, giving you online privacy and protecting sensitive data.

6.6. Regular Data Backup

The importance of regularly backing up your data cannot be overstated. Regardless of all preventative measures, accidents can occur, data losses can happen due to hardware malfunctions or malware attacks. Regular backups ensure that you can restore your data, keeping your digital life intact.

6.7. Social Media Privacy Settings

Finally, closely monitor your social media privacy settings. Social platforms are often the most targeted due to the wealth of easily exploitable personal data. By disciplining oneself to limit sharing personal information and utilizing privacy settings effectively, you can prevent unnecessary exposure, thus securing your social media presence.

In sum, securing your digital life is not an optional luxury but an inherent necessity. As you interact more with the digital world, as your digital footprint grows, it becomes increasingly relevant to commit to the safety measures outlined in this chapter. These methods and tools, coupled with a consciousness of the potential online threats, can ensure a safer journey in the digital world. By integrating these practices into your daily routine, you can confidently engage online with relative peace of mind, knowing you've taken substantial steps to protect your digital legacy.

Chapter 7. Embarking on a Digital Detox: Benefits and Strategies

In the modern era, where digital devices dominate our routines and entangle us in the web of incessant communication and information exchange, taking a breather, a sabbatical from this digital inundation often becomes a necessity rather than a choice. An effective way to regain control over your digital existence and restore your mental tranquility is a digital detox – a conscious and deliberate disconnection from the digital world for a prescribed period. This chapter will delve into the concept of a digital detox, its benefits, and strategies for successful execution.

7.1. The Concept and Necessity of a Digital Detox

A digital detox refers to a temporary or occasional pause taken from the usage of digital devices, especially those providing access to the Internet, notably smartphones, computers, and tablets. It is a buffer period that excludes all forms of emails, social media, digital news, and online shopping. A digital detox is not about vilifying technology; it is about creating a balance.

In a world where more than 3.5 billion people own a smartphone and average screen time often surpasses 6 hours a day, digital detoxification becomes a necessity. It strikes the right balance between dense usage and oversaturation, preventing digital burnout. In modern parlance, it's like the oil to the machinery of our lives, ensuring the gears run smoothly without diastrous overheating.

7.2. The Enormous Benefits of a Digital Detox

Disconnecting from the digital world comes with a multitude of benefits. These span from seeing improvements in mental health to enhanced-consciousness towards our surroundings.

1. Enhanced Focus and Productivity: Without the beep of notifications or the urge to scroll through social media feeds, you will notice a remarkable increase in your attention span. You would be able to work on tasks without getting distracted every few minutes, leading to significant improvements in both productivity and performance.

2. Mental Well-being: Constantly being online can lead to a surge of information that our brains are not designed to handle, often leading to feelings of overwhelm, stress, and anxiety. Digital detox can reduce the pressure of immediate responsiveness promoted by social media, enabling better emotional health.

3. Improved Physical Health: Extended digital device usage leads to sedentary behavior, fostering a slew of health issues like obesity, cardiovascular disease, and even eyesight problems. A digital detox can get your blood flowing again and break the chain of sedentary lifestyle patterns.

4. Better Inter-personal Relationships: Digital detox allows for greater interaction with your family and community. People often notice deeper satisfaction in their relationships as they are better able to engage without the interference of digital distractions.

5. Nature Reconnection: Removing digital distractions opens a window to reconnect with nature and our natural circadian rhythms, promoting both emotional and physical well-being.

7.3. Execution Strategies for a Successful Digital Detox

Executing a successful digital detox requires more than just the will to disconnect. It is a careful orchestration of pre-planned strategies that reinforce our commitment to this detox—and here are some of these essential strategies.

1. Setting Clear Boundaries: Know what you are taking a detox from: Is it work emails, social media, or news websites? Defining these boundaries will help you maintain the structure of your detoxification process.

2. Establishing a Time Period: Be clear with how long you want to disconnect. This could be anything from a few hours every day to a week or months. Make sure the duration suits your lifestyle and responsibilities and is not a cause for additional stress.

3. Communication is Key: Let your friends, family, and colleagues know about your digital detox. This ensures that they are aware of your unavailability and can adjust their expectations accordingly.

4. Plan Alternatives: With the void that digital disconnection leaves, you must plan alternative activities. It could be catching up on reading, learning a new hobby, or some form of physical activity.

5. Gradual Weaning Off: If letting go cold turkey seems daunting, consider gradually decreasing your digital time until it feels manageable.

6. Seeking Help: Consider turning to professionals or joining a support group if you struggle with the detox. Remember, help is always available.

Adopting a digital detox is not about abandoning technology; rather, it is about shaping its usage scope to complement our lives instead of controlling them. As you embark on this journey, summon the strength to stay committed, conquer digital dependence, and reclaim your life away from the screen. You've got a universe to explore outside the digital realm, a world that cannot be contained within pixels of a screen, but draws its essence from your senses and experiences. Let the digital detox be the blueprint for a lifestyle where you wield the power, not your devices. Enjoy the process, learn through the challenges, and emerge triumphantly, ready to define the paths for your digital footprint. With this, you won't just restore balance but will also take a seminal step towards shaping your digital legacy.

Chapter 8. Managing Your Micro-moments: From Posts to Stories

In the orbits of the digital universe, your interactions, activities, and attitudes transform into minuscule yet substantial 'micro-moments'. These are tiny snippets of your digital journey that habitually stitch a broader narrative of your online persona. From quick posts or tweets to the entrancing Instagram or Snapchat stories – the digital realm enables you to create and share in real-time, thereby augmenting the volumes of your digital repository.

8.1. The Essence of Micro-moments

Micro-moments are described as the intuitive, reflexive instances wherein users turn to a digital device, primarily a smartphone, to act on an immediate need or whim. We reach for these devices when we want to know, go, do, or buy something - or simply for sharing an emotion, an event, or a life update. Through these actions, you are exposing the essence of your life to the world, depositing nuggets of your existence into the infinite warehouses of internet data.

Yet, we often fail to recognize the intricate line between sharing and oversharing. Unrestrained or frivolous sharing can lead to divulging personal information, may incite unnecessary debates or controversies, and even dilute or discolor your digital persona. Hence, managing your micro-moments efficaciously is an art that requires a delicate balance between amplifying your life's high points and withholding anything too private or inappropriate.

8.2. From Posts to Stories

Facebook posts, Instagram stories, Twitter tweets, LinkedIn updates - all of them encapsulate your 'micro-moments.' In this section, we'll delve into how to strike a delicate balance while tactfully managing these online narratives.

Facebook and LinkedIn Posts: These platforms offer a more formal, professional space for sharing your thoughts, opinions, experiences, and achievements. Be mindful of the content and language you use here. Maintain a polite, respectful tone devoid of any controversial or contentious statements. Ensure that your posts align with your professional goals and personal values.

Instagram and Snapchat Stories: These present a more casual, personal space where you can showcase your creativity, hobbies, travel, events, accomplishments, and more. You can use filters, stickers, texts, and other tools to make your content attractive and engaging. However, ensure you share only appropriate content that you are comfortable with the world seeing and remembering.

8.3. Creating Engaging and Safe Content

Ensuring that your micro-moments not only resonate with your persona but are also secure is crucial. Follow these simple guidelines for safe and engaging content creation:

Privacy Settings: Regularly check and update your privacy settings as per your comfort level, remembering that setting conducive privacy safeguards is of paramount importance.

Think Before You Share: Reflect on the content you are about to post and its potential implications. Could it be misconstrued, controversial, or inappropriate? If the answer is 'yes' or 'maybe,' it might be prudent to reconsider.

Respect Others' Privacy: When sharing content involving other people - friends, coworkers, family members - always seek their consent before posting.

Engage Responsibly: Be respectful in your interactions. Avoid internet arguments or posting disproportionally emotional content, which could lead to misunderstandings or complications.

Use Strong, Unique Passwords: Protecting your accounts from hacking is vital. Use strong, unique passwords and two-factor authentication where applicable.

By adhering to the above guidelines, you can successfully manage your online presence and digital interactions, converting these micro-moments into a constructive, pleasant, and safe digital journey.

8.4. The Power and Peril of Micro-moments

Recognize the enormity entrenched within these fleeting digital encounters. Each micro-moment carries the potential to either reinforce or dismantle your online image. At their best, these instants can offer unique insights into your life, endearing moments of authenticity, and opportunities for genuine connection. Yet, they can also expose vulnerabilities, stir controversies, or present an unfiltered, thoughtless glimpse into your life that might invite unnecessary scrutiny or judgement.

Therefore, it's about being conscious and conscientious of these valuable micro-moments that dot your digital landscape. Convert each post or story into an instrument of positive online persona building. Make each shared micro-moment count towards leaving an indelible yet intentional digital footprint, thereby fashioning an online legacy that truly resonates with who you are.

Remember, you are the curator of your digital life, the actor, and the narrator. Decrypting the nuances of these micro-moments and managing them astutely can empower you to elegantly script your digital story.

Chapter 9. The Legality of Digital Legacy: Getting to Know Your Rights

Navigating the rapidly evolving digital landscape is akin to navigating a legal minefield, with every user action potentially interacting with regulations and laws. This predominance of legal considerations underscores the immense importance of understanding the legal aspects of your digital legacy.

9.1. The Legal Landscape of the Digital World

The virtual space has dissolved geographical boundaries, meaning that users from across the globe interact with each other like never before. This inevitably spells the interaction of diverse legal systems and principles. From copyright laws that regulate your creative content to privacy regulations that govern how much of your information can be accessed and by whom, the digital world is a complicated sphere where one's actions may have far-reaching legal implications.

Exploring this realm demands for an understanding of some key legal concepts. From varying data protection and privacy laws, to regulations about freedom of speech versus defamation, it becomes evident that awareness of the legal dimensions of our digital behavior is not just an intellectual curiosity, it is an absolute necessity.

Copyright laws and intellectual property rights come into conversation quite frequently when discussing digital legacy. The online content you create, whether it's a brilliant piece of code, a riveting blog post, or a captivating graphic design, can be protected by these laws. Similarly, ensuring you respect others' digital rights is essential to prevent facing legal consequences.

9.2. Your Rights & Responsibilities

When you create content online and share it, you're protected by various international intellectual property laws. However, understanding this legal paradigm requires managing a careful balance between protecting your rights and demonstrating due respect for others'.

You bear the responsibility to treat others' digital content with respect. This means not using or sharing content without proper authorization, particularly content under copyright protection. Disregarding these legalities can lead to nasty lawsuits that involve fines and, in serious cases, even jail time. What's more, it may tarnish your overall digital legacy – a cost that is perhaps the most damaging to your online reputation.

9.3. Privacy & Data Protection Laws

Beyond rights and responsibilities related to content, your digital legacy also implicates privacy and data protection laws. Globally diverse privacy laws dictate how your personal data is accessed, used, and protected. If you have international outreach, you may also have to grapple with international data protection regulations like the General Data Protection Regulation (GDPR) or the California Consumer Privacy Act (CCPA). These laws provide directive and protection for users against the unauthorized use and distribution of their personal data.

Data protection laws can also confer you with certain rights, including the right to access data held about you, rectify data if it is inaccurate, or delete your data altogether (the 'right to be forgotten').

Understanding these laws and effectively enforcing your rights could have a profound impact on your digital legacy.

9.4. Legal Considerations Post-Mortem

But what happens to your digital legacy after your death? Death is an inevitable part of life and planning for it, including what happens to your digital assets, is something that needs to be considered.

Digital wills and heirs are becoming increasingly common, allowing users to dictate who gets access to their online accounts (email, social media, etc.) after death. Several laws and regulations dictate how these digital assets should be handled and transferred post-mortem, and knowing them is indispensable for planning a smooth transition.

Notably, social media platforms usually have policies in place to manage the accounts of deceased users. If you want someone to manage your account after you die, you'll need to appoint a Legacy Contact, Online Executor, or similar role, and the requirements vary per platform.

9.5. Steps Towards Legal Vigilance

In conclusion, the legality of a digital legacy involves understanding the multiplicity of laws and regulations that govern the digital sphere, from copyright to privacy protection laws. Going forward, the paramount step should be to ensure that your digital interactions (both consumption and creation) are legally sound and respectful of others' rights.

It might appear quite daunting, but law's detailed and complicated nature shouldn't deter us from aiming to understand it better. Knowing your rights and the legislative landscape is the first step towards ensuring a respectful, protected, and enduring digital legacy.

Many useful resources, advisory bodies, and digital legacy services can help you navigate this complex journey, so you're not in it alone.

Let your digital footprint be a testament to your respect for the law, and tread cautiously in the face of potential legal ramifications. Our digital realm fosters connections and promotes creativity, but it requires us to be vigilant custodians of our own digital legacies. After all, the law is there to protect us, and knowing how to wield it is a powerful step in creating a durable, respectful, and lasting digital path.

Chapter 10. Digital Heirs: Safeguarding Your Digital Trails

Understanding the increasing overlap of our physical and digital lives is key to comprehending the importance of digital heirs in safeguarding your digital trails. As one walks the labyrinth of cyberspace, the footprints left in forms of accounts, messages, uploaded pictures and documents, statuses, and posts accumulate to form a digital legacy. Like any legacy, these trails can carry immense value, demanding diligent guarding and careful transfer to the rightful inheritors, your digital heirs.

10.1. The Importance of Designating Digital Heirs

Designating digital heirs is paramount to maintaining your digital autonomy beyond your physical existence. Digital heirs are individuals entrusted with your digital assets. These digital assets can range from financial holdings in electronic wallets to a collection of e-books, from treasured memories captured and posted on social media to essential documents stored in the cloud. But perhaps the most crucial of these are the pieces of you embedded in the digital words you've written, the media you've created, or the digital conversations you've been a part of. Fail to designate your digital heirs, and these pieces of you may be left stranded, unattended, or worse yet, appropriated by unscrupulous individuals.

10.2. How to Choose Your Digital Heirs

Choosing your digital heirs is a highly personal process. The involved individuals should be trustworthy, able to navigate digital platforms comfortably, and ideally, understanding of your digital inclinations and wishes. Sometimes, it may be prudent to designate different heirs for various types of digital assets, dependent on their importance, the sensitivity of the information contained, or the digital competency required to manage them.

10.3. Defining Digital Assets

Before we delve further into the digital inheritance process, let's demarcate what digital assets are. They can be tangible, intangible, personal, or financial, but they exist in the digital realm. They can include:

- Digital devices: Computers, smartphones, hard drives, etc.

- Online accounts: Emails, social networks, cloud storage, etc.

- Digital collections: E-books, music, video files, photographs, etc.

- Digital currency: Bitcoin, Ethereum, etc.

- Online financial accounts: PayPal, online banking, investment platforms, etc.

Managing these diverse types of digital assets is challenging, making the nomination and guidance of digital heirs important for a smoother transition.

10.4. Creating a Digital Will

The cornerstone of safeguarding digital trails is a well-drafted digital will. It should include an exhaustive list of your digital assets along with login credentials, security questions, and other necessary details required for access. This should be accompanied by clear instructions regarding how you would like each of these assets to be handled upon your death.

Digital wills also need to be updated regularly to remain relevant, reflecting changes in your digital property and variations in your preferences over time. Relying on professional expertise for this task ensures robust, legally compliant terms that can avoid potential future disputes.

10.5. Legal Implications and Challenges

While the idea of protecting and passing on one's digital legacy has gained ground, the legal landscape around it is still sketchy in many parts of the world. While some countries have regulations respecting digital wills and digital heirs, many do not. Even where laws exist, digital inheritance is often rife with jurisdictional intricacies given the cross-border nature of much of our digital lives and the varied legal approaches globally.

10.6. Engaging with Service Providers

The terms of service provided by various digital service platforms can also significantly dictate the control of your digital legacy. Some platforms offer inheritance options, like Facebook's 'Legacy Contact' or Google's 'Inactive Account Manager.' These features often allow for limited account management by the digital heir after death or account inactivity, which can be hugely beneficial if planned for in advance.

Finally, it's crucial to communicate your plans and intentions with your designated digital heirs. Making them aware of their responsibilities, the needed wherewithal, and the sentiment behind this digital inheritance can go a long way in ensuring that your digital remnants will be maintained, cherished, remembered, or even deleted, exactly as you desired.

The landscape of digital legacy safeguards is continually evolving. As technology advances and our digital footprints expand, it's more important than ever to think about our digital heirs and ensure they're prepared to shoulder our digital legacies. It's an essential component of managing your digital life and leaving a positive, enduring virtual footprint. As such, learning to navigate digital inheritance adequately is indeed a skill for the present and the future.

Chapter 11. The Future of Digital Footprints: Trends and Forecasts

As we crest the peak of the digital era, primed to plunge into the vivid prospects of cyberspace, it is paramount to glean insights about the demographic shifts, technological innovations, legal frameworks and global trends shaping the future of digital footprints. A thorough understanding of these dynamics can not only guide us to navigate the virtual landscapes with prudent diligence but can also help us predict, and potentially inform, the future trajectory of digital identities.

11.1. The Evolution of Digital Avatars

Initially, digital footprints were mere reflections of offline identities—rigid and skeletal. Websites, accounts, and profiles were like online business cards, chiefly used professional engagements. But now, digital footprints have evolved into dynamic avatars, shadowing our real selves comprehensively and perpetually into the cyber realm.

Emergent technologies like Artificial Intelligence (AI), Virtual Reality (VR), Internet of Things (IoT), and blockchain are revolutionizing the maintenance, expansion, and security of digital footprints. As AI becomes more capable of mimicking human behavior, the line between users and their digital representations are blurring. VR is transforming the experience of digital footprints from a two-dimensional space to a multi-dimensional one, opening doors to immersive and interactive pearls of virtual experiences. Blockchain technology, using its prerogative of decentralization and security, ensures that your digital footprint remains immutable and solely under your possession.

11.2. Digital Footprints and Regulations

On a global scale, governments are becoming increasingly aware of the implications of digital footprints. There's a growing concern for protecting individuals' virtual identities, with legislations like the General Data Protection Regulation (GDPR) in the European Union, and the California Consumer Privacy Act (CCPA) enacted to safeguard individual online privacy.

Forthcoming regulations will probably walk the tightrope between securing personal information and maintaining the free speech ethos of the internet. Since digital footprints play a pivotal role in forensic investigations, anti-terrorist operations, and criminal tracking, the regulatory landscape will likely strive to strike a balance between privacy preservation and security enforcement.

11.3. Shifting User Behavior

Modern internet users are growing more cognizant of their digital footprints and the attached implications. Pioneering research indicates an intentional digital footprint reduction trend, fueled by privacy concerns and desires for digital detoxification.

Future users might curate their online personas more mindfully, creating tailored footprints for different online platforms. While your professional footprint may shine on LinkedIn, your hobby-oriented persona might express itself through Instagram. Understanding these nuances will be vital for strategic digital interactions, and successful outreach and engagement in an increasingly segmented cyber environment.

11.4. The Specter of Digital Afterlife

As our digital footprints enlarge, so does the grave reality of managing these expanses post-mortem. Death in the digital age means coping with the virtual remains of our departed loved ones and our own digital assets once we're gone.

The concept of 'digital heirs,' individuals assigned to manage your online affairs after death, is gaining traction. Services like Facebook's legacy contact, Google's Inactive Account Manager, and various digital will services are the vanguard of this discourse. This, inevitably, will become a significant part of our digital futures, as more individuals plan for their virtual demise as meticulously as their tangible one.

11.5. Forecasts and Implications

The surface of the terra incognita of the future of digital footprints is merely grazed here. While the explosive growth of the digital society promises an exhilarating future, it also brings forth significant challenges. Technological advances and shifting user behaviors will interplay with regulatory landscapes, shaping the future evolution of our digital identities.

In this dynamic online ecosystem, it's critical to remain proactive, adaptable, and informed. As we saddle up to plunge into the future of digital footprints, it is essential to periodically reevaluate and recalibrate our strategies, enabling us to not just survive, but ostensibly influence the virtual narrative of the morrow. The symphony of our digital stories, told through the echoes of our footprints, will resound in the infiniteness of cyberspace, painting portraits of our individual selves with the brushstrokes of our digital interactions.